Lead from Behind

Why True Leaders Put People First

A.T. RAMOS

© [2024] A. T. RAMOS. All rights reserved.

No part of this publication may be reproduced, distributed, or transmitted in any form or by any means, including photocopying, recording, or other electronic or mechanical methods, without the prior written permission of the author, except in the case of brief quotations embodied in reviews and certain noncommercial uses permitted by copyright law.

Lead from Behind

Contents

Introduction: 5

The Importance of Leadership from Behind 5

Why the Conventional Leadership Model Is Losing Its Advantage ... 7

    How Does It Look to Lead from Behind? 9

    Examples of Leading from Behind in the Real World 11

    Why It's Better to Lead from Behind in the Modern World 13

    The Path Ahead: The Need for More Leaders Who Take the Lead 15

(Section I:) 17

The Theory of Leading from the Back 17

    1. Comprehending the Idea 17

    2. The Reason It Works 20

(Section II:) 26

Fundamentals of Leading from Behind 26

    3. Power Over Authority 26

    4. Developing Powerful Connections 29

    5. Prioritizing others is the essence of servant leadership. 33

    6. Paying More Attention Than Talking 36

(Section III:) 40

Practical Leadership from Behind 40

    7. Fostering Creativity and Innovation. 40

Lead from Behind

    8. Effective Delegation 43

    9. Managing Emergency Conditions 46

    10. Developing the Next Wave of Leaders 50

(Section IV:) 55

Prospects for Leadership 55

    11. Redefining Success: The Team, Not You, is the Key. 55

    12. Establishing a Durable Legacy 59

Conclusion: The Way Ahead 64

    Empowerment Tools 66

    Creating a Helpful Network 68

    Developing the Upcoming Leadership Generation 70

    The trip goes on 71

Introduction:

The Importance of Leadership from Behind

It's customary to think of leadership as a bold, visible individual at the forefront who commands attention and leads the charge into new territory. The hero who stands tall, gives commands, and urges others to follow him is the picture that is entrenched in our sense of leadership. For millennia, the "leader-as-commander" archetype has affected political arenas, company boardrooms, and even personal development stories. However, as the world evolves, so too must our understanding of successful leadership.

Lead from Behind

For a long time, authority, control, and an emphasis on personal charisma have been connected to the conventional "top-down" leadership method. But what if being the first person to cross the finish line or the loudest voice in the room isn't what true leadership is all about? What if the most influential leaders are those that stand behind their colleagues, not in front of them, and gently help others achieve?

This is the principle of leading from behind, which prioritizes others and lets them take center stage while the leader gently supports their success in the background. Instead of dominance and control, this style of leadership stresses support, empowerment, and trust. Instead of focusing just on individual accomplishments, it stresses the growth and development of others, utilizing the team's collective strength. By doing this, leadership from behind not only delivers better results but also cultivates more substantial and long-lasting benefits on both individuals and organizations.

This chapter will discuss why this method is more successful as well as more pertinent in the interrelated and multifaceted world of today. You will learn why stepping back can frequently be the most effective move a leader can make through anecdotes of outstanding leaders who have perfected the art of leading from behind and real-world situations that highlight the advantages of this paradigm.

Why the Conventional Leadership Model Is Losing Its Advantage

We have been indoctrinated for years to honor a particular type of leader. These are the vivacious visionaries, the charming folks who seem to know everything, and they are the ones that command their companies with a strong will and aggressiveness. They are frequently referred to as "command and control" leaders because they are in charge, act rapidly, and insist that their people follow out their objectives without question.

There is no doubting that this practice has helped some people succeed. Leaders like General George S. Patton, whose strong military leadership won World War II, or Steve Jobs, whose unflinching vision for Apple reshaped the digital sector, are commonly cited as the ideal. Leaders who are directive, loud, and in the spotlight are easy to identify and even easier to appreciate.

However, things have changed. The majority of teams don't react well to authoritarian control, and the workplace is no longer a fight. More dynamic, cooperative, and inclusive settings are replacing the tight hierarchies of the past. People are no longer satisfied with merely following orders without having a say in the process, companies are flatter, and communication can go in many different directions. When multiple opinions are valued and teamwork is stressed, innovation flourishes rather than when one individual decides the course.

The advantages of the top-down technique are beginning to erode. Today's workforce values empowerment, autonomy, and purpose. They are searching for leaders who listen, who are responsive to new ideas, and who create environments where everyone can contribute their all. Leading from behind becomes important in this situation rather than merely a nice characteristic.

How Does It Look to Lead from Behind?

Being a leader from behind does not imply a lack of accountability or leadership. It's not about avoiding decision-making or being passive. Rather, it's about acknowledging that leadership is a shared obligation and that allowing others take initiative is frequently the ideal way to lead.

Consider being a shepherd to be like leading from behind. A shepherd does not lead the flock by walking in front of them and tugging them along, nor does he sit by and let them wander aimlessly. Rather, he follows in his wake, monitoring, leading, and guarding. When needed, he gently prods the flock to stay on course, but generally lets them go at their own speed. The flock—making sure that every sheep finds its way safely is the important issue, not the shepherd.

An atmosphere where people feel empowered to take responsibility for their task is likewise established by a leader who leads from behind. They do not control the process; rather, they function as facilitators, giving their team the tools, direction, and support they need to succeed. They acknowledge the group's accomplishments as well as their own.

Examples of Leading from Behind in the Real World

This philosophy is exemplified by many of the most well-known and affluent leaders of today. Consider Nelson Mandela, for instance. Mandela is frequently referred to be the classic leader from behind. It is better to lead from behind and put people in front, especially when you celebrate victory when wonderful things happen, he famously observed. In times of danger, you take the front line. People will then respect your leadership.

Mandela did not try to force his will on the South African public while he was in government. Rather, he encouraged communication, supported peace, and offered people the tools they needed to repair the country. Even if it meant stepping out of

Lead from Behind

the spotlight, he knew that true leadership meant providing room for others to contribute.

Contemporary business leadership provides yet another striking example. Take Microsoft CEO Satya Nadella, for example. Many individuals believe that Nadella changed Microsoft's culture from one of harshness and rivalry to one of openness and cooperation. He advocated listening, empathy, and inclusivity—qualities that are needed for a leader who takes the lead. Microsoft has developed swiftly under his supervision, not because he pressed his own agenda but rather because he offered everyone in the firm the freedom to be creative and accept responsibility for their work.

These pictures underline a vital feature of leading from behind: it has nothing to do with the leader's celebrity or money. It's about establishing an atmosphere that allows others to develop, frequently in ways that are greater than the leader's own personal potential. The emphasis moves from "What can I accomplish? to "What are we able to accomplish together?"

Why It's Better to Lead from Behind in the Modern World

The age in which we live is one of complexity. The problems that communities, organizations, and even individuals face are complex and call for a variety of viewpoints, abilities, and concepts. No matter how intelligent or skilled a leader is, they cannot possibly know everything. The idea that one person should know everything is actually out of date and ineffective.

In a society where creativity and teamwork are essential, a leader's job is to foster an environment where solutions can arise rather than to prescribe them. Leaders who take the back seat know that their role is to create an atmosphere where everyone can contribute to the group's success, not to play the hero. In addition to producing superior outcomes, this strengthens, engages, and fortifies the team.

The focus on emotional intelligence and empathy is one of the most crucial elements of leading from behind. IQ intelligence, strategy, and vision—was frequently the center of traditional leadership. But in today's environment, emotional intelligence is just as, if not more, crucial. Leaders who are sympathetic and who understand the emotional needs of their team members can build deeper connections, foster greater loyalty, and create a more supportive work environment.

Moreover, leading from behind creates a sense of ownership and accountability among the team. When people feel empowered to take charge of their job, they are more likely to be interested, motivated, and invested in the outcomes. They perform better and are more satisfied when they feel appreciated and trusted.

The Path Ahead: The Need for More Leaders Who Take the Lead

The demand for leaders who can lead from behind will only increase as the twenty-first century progresses. The difficulties we face—whether in industry, government, or society at large—are too complicated and too interwoven to be solved by a single person or a small number of persons. We require leaders who can harness the potential of the group, foster an atmosphere that encourages innovation, and give others the confidence to take charge and lead independently.

Giving up power or avoiding accountability is not the goal of leading from behind. It's about understanding that real leadership is about helping others, empowering them, and fostering an environment where they can thrive. It's about realizing that the most effective leaders are those who quietly, carefully, and humbly lead from behind rather than those who command from the front.

We will go deeper into the ideas and methods of leading from behind in the upcoming chapters, providing useful tactics, real-world examples, and actionable insights that you can use in your own leadership development. The lessons of leading from behind will help you become the kind of leader that not only succeeds but also leaves a legacy of empowerment and long-lasting influence, regardless of how many people you are leading two hundred or two hundred.

(Section I:)

The Theory of Leading from the Back

1. Comprehending the Idea

The concept of leading from behind might appear paradoxical at first. After all, boldness, authority, and visibility are frequently linked to leadership. We see leaders as individuals who take the stage, motivating their groups with stirring speeches, setting an example for others to follow, and making choices that affect the organization as a whole. Leading from behind, however, challenges us to rethink what it means to be a leader.

Lead from Behind

Leading from behind is an active and deliberate decision to empower people while offering support and direction from a more subdued position; it is not about being passive. The origins of this idea can be found in a number of different civilizations and philosophical systems. The ancient Chinese philosopher Lao Tzu, for instance, highlighted the value of selflessness and humility in leadership. He maintained that the greatest leaders are those who serve their people in his foundational work, the Tao Te Ching, and that the ideal kind of ruler is one whose existence is hardly acknowledged by the populace.

Similarly, leaders like Mahatma Gandhi and Nelson Mandela demonstrated leading from behind by putting the good of the group ahead of their own power. They understood that genuine leadership is about creating an atmosphere where people may flourish rather than using force to control others. Mandela's strategy during South Africa's post-apartheid transition placed a strong emphasis on empowerment, inclusivity, and communication, facilitating a peaceful change while empowering people to take charge of their own destiny.

What distinguishes traditional leadership styles from leading from behind, then? The main difference is how the leader handles power and influence. A front-line leader frequently exhibits a command-and-control mentality, attempting to force their will and vision on the others. A leader who leads from behind, on the other hand, takes a more cooperative approach, promoting team member involvement and facilitating debates. People feel free to express their opinions and take chances without worrying about failing because of this distinction, which fosters a culture of psychological safety and trust.

Sadly, there are still false beliefs about leading from behind. This strategy could be interpreted by some as being weak or unfocused. Some might see it as a way to escape accountability. But it takes a great deal of bravery and self-awareness to lead from behind. It requires a thorough comprehension of team dynamics as well as the capacity to actively listen, pose insightful queries, and offer assistance when required. This leadership style is based on the understanding that although leaders may pilot the ship, the crew is ultimately responsible for guiding it to success.

2. The Reason It Works

Numerous organizational and psychological elements that support a more creative and motivated workforce are responsible for the efficacy of leading from behind. Fundamentally, this leadership approach encourages a climate of trust and cooperation, which makes it easier for people to cooperate more successfully in pursuit of shared objectives.

Building team trust is one of the main psychological advantages of leading from behind. Leaders that take on a supporting position convey that they have faith in their team's talents. This idea promotes psychological safety, where people can freely share their ideas and opinions without worrying about criticism or retaliation. Google's Project Aristotle research indicates that teams with high psychological safety continuously perform better than those with lower levels of trust. When team members feel encouraged, they are more willing to take chances, provide creative ideas, and grow from their errors.

Additionally, leading from behind promotes teamwork and group problem-solving. In a conventional top-down leadership approach, the leader is frequently the only one who can make decisions. This may result in lost chances for insightful opinions and suggestions from team members who might possess special knowledge and viewpoints. A leader who promotes collaboration, on the other hand, invites a variety of viewpoints to be heard, which leads to more creative ideas and greater team support.

This focus on teamwork is consistent with the contemporary view of leadership as a shared duty. Leaders must foster an atmosphere where everyone feels empowered to contribute in a time when firms are depending more and more on cross-functional collaboration and teamwork. By shifting the emphasis from individual achievements to group success, leading from behind fosters a sense of shared accountability and ownership among team members.

Furthermore, leading from behind fosters a culture of ongoing development and learning. Leaders that put their team's development first inspire others to take charge of their own educational paths. Leaders can serve as facilitators by pointing team members in the direction of resources, offering helpful criticism, and promoting experimentation rather than offering all the solutions. This strategy not only encourages personal development but also increases the team's ability to adjust and come up with new ideas when faced with obstacles.

Additionally, leading from behind promotes flexibility in a dynamic setting. Organizations need to be able to quickly adapt to new information, changes in the market, and emerging technology in today's fast-paced world. By empowering their team to be proactive and responsive, a leader who leads from behind facilitates quicker decision-making and greater adaptability. Team members are more likely to take the initiative and make decisions when they feel empowered and trusted, which makes the organization more flexible.

In conclusion, leading from behind is a philosophy based on empowerment, trust, and teamwork rather than merely being a new style of leadership. Leaders may foster an atmosphere where people feel appreciated and inspired to give their all by putting others' success first. This change in viewpoint results in more involvement, better performance, and an innovative culture that is advantageous to all parties.

As we delve deeper into the fundamentals of leading from behind, we'll unearth useful tactics and takeaways that will enable you to accept this idea and successfully implement it in your own leadership development. In addition to changing the leader, adopting the strategy of leading from behind can improve the organization as a whole and promote a collaborative and shared success culture, which is crucial for negotiating the challenges of the contemporary world.

Call to action

Appreciate you reading! I would want to take a moment to personally thank you for selecting to read my work. Your time and effort are much valued; perhaps, this book will give you insightful analysis and successful techniques.

Your comments are very much valued as I develop as an author. I would love to hear your thoughts—whether positive or constructive so I can improve and make future works even more helpful and engaging.

 I respectfully ask that you write an honest review whether you thought this book was beneficial or if you could see anything improved. Your observations will not only help me but also guide other readers toward appropriate materials.

I appreciate your support once more; I am looking forward your comments. Good wishes,

(Section II:)

Fundamentals of Leading from Behind

3. Power Over Authority

The proverb "knowledge is power" frequently translates into control in the context of leadership. Many CEOs think that maintaining tight control will guarantee their organization's success. However, this paradigm is reversed when one leads from behind. Giving workers the freedom to take charge and lead in their positions not only promotes a feeling of community but also stimulates creativity and output.

Leaders who embrace empowerment foster an atmosphere in which staff members are comfortable taking chances and making decisions. Giving up micromanagement, a typical mistake made by many leaders who are afraid of losing control, is necessary for this change. Micromanagement has the potential to discourage innovation, demoralize workers, and ultimately impede the advancement of the company. Leaders should trust their teams and give them the freedom to experiment with different ideas and methods rather than micromanaging every work.

Take Google, which is well known for its inventive culture, as an example. As a result of the company's policy permitting employees to dedicate 20% of their workweek to personal projects, successful products such as Google News and Gmail have been developed. Google has fostered an environment where creativity flourishes by allowing its employees to follow their passions. Leaders need to understand that they are not the only ones with solutions and that their staff frequently have special insights that help advance the company.

The development of leadership abilities inside the team is another aspect of empowerment. Fostering a culture of accountability and shared responsibility can be achieved by encouraging staff members to assume leadership responsibilities, even if they are modest. Team members can be given the chance to chair meetings, direct projects, or serve as mentors by their leaders. As people start to see themselves as essential to the success of the company, this not only improves their abilities but also fortifies the team dynamic.

Leaders should place a high priority on open communication in order to promote empowerment. Creating avenues for communication and feedback enables staff members to express their thoughts, worries, and goals. Team members are more likely to put their all into their work and make a significant contribution to the objectives of the company when they feel heard. Empowerment calls for constant encouragement and support; it is not a one-time event. Leaders need to constantly evaluate how they may inspire their teams to be proactive, innovative, and take on leadership positions.

In conclusion, allowing workers more autonomy over their workplace produces a vibrant environment that stimulates innovation and engagement. Leaders that take a stance of trust and support empower their colleagues to stand up and unlock potential that can result in extraordinary results.

4. Developing Powerful Connections

The power of connection is at the core of good leadership. Developing solid connections based on trust and empathy is an essential part of leading from behind; it is not merely an aspirational concept. The capacity to create enduring relationships with team members distinguishes outstanding leaders in the fast-paced, frequently impersonal commercial world of today.

Sincere empathy is the foundation of healthy partnerships. The capacity to comprehend and experience another person's emotions is known as empathy. Leaders show that they care about their team members' well-being in addition to their performance when they take the time to get to know them personally. This relationship builds trust and creates an environment where workers feel appreciated and understood.

Building relationships requires active participation. Instead of only checking in with their team members at meetings or performance assessments, leaders should try to do so on a frequent basis. Asking someone how their weekend was or showing interest in their career aspirations are simple yet effective ways to build connection.

These exchanges foster a feeling of community and break down barriers among the team.

Once built, trust serves as a basis for cooperation. Members of a team who have faith in their leader are more inclined to express their opinions, raise issues, and provide helpful criticism. By listening to and acting upon this feedback, a leader shows their team that they appreciate their opinions, which further cements their relationship. Because they know their leader has their back, people feel free to take chances and be creative in an atmosphere of trust.

Furthermore, solid bonds go beyond the leader-team interaction. In order to create an inclusive culture where cooperation thrives, effective leaders promote team spirit. Formal or informal team-building exercises can improve connections between coworkers. Team members are more inclined to collaborate and use one another's abilities to accomplish shared objectives when they have a personal connection.

Vulnerability is a key component of developing healthy connections. Leaders who are open about their own struggles, setbacks, and experiences foster a real environment. Team members are encouraged to talk about their difficulties because they know they are not alone because of this vulnerability. Sharing personal tales strengthens bonds and underlines that leadership is about development and resiliency rather than perfection.

In the end, it is impossible to overestimate the significance of empathy, connection, and trust in leadership. Better teamwork, increased morale, and increased employee engagement are all correlated with strong relationships. By putting these values first, leaders foster an environment where people are encouraged to give their all because they know they are appreciated and supported.

5. Prioritizing others is the essence of servant leadership.

This idea is central to servant leadership, a philosophy that prioritizes putting people first, as the adage goes, "a rising tide lifts all boats." Because they understand that their success is closely tied to the success of the company, servant leaders put their team members' growth and development ahead of results at the price of employee well-being.

The conventional perspective of leadership as a top-down, hierarchical approach is contested by servant leadership. Rather, it encourages the notion that leaders are there to support their teams and enable them to reach their greatest potential. Because it places a strong emphasis on teamwork, empathy, and shared responsibility, this strategy is consistent with the ideas of leading from behind.

A fundamental principle of servant leadership is the dedication to fostering each person's unique abilities. Understanding each team member's distinct skills and interests is a top priority for leaders who embrace this attitude. Leaders foster an atmosphere where workers feel appreciated and involved by identifying and fostering these strengths. People are more likely to feel satisfied with their jobs and take responsibility for their work when they are given the freedom to participate in ways that play to their strengths.

Servant leaders actively foster their team members' professional and personal growth in addition to fostering their strengths. This assistance can come in many forms, such as offering tools for developing one's skills or promoting career progression. Leaders create a culture of learning and development that benefits both individuals and the company overall by making investments in the professional development of their staff.

Additionally, servant leadership highlights the value of cooperation and community. In order for people to feel connected and supported, leaders should try to foster a sense of belonging within their teams. In addition to raising staff morale, this sense of community promotes cooperation and teamwork. Team members are more likely to actively support the organization's mission when they believe they are a part of something bigger than themselves.

Although putting people first is crucial, servant leadership also recognizes the significance of outcomes. The difference, though, is in how those outcomes are attained. Servant leaders foster an atmosphere where people are inspired to give their best work by putting their teams' welfare first. Employees are more likely to be engaged and productive when they feel appreciated and supported, which eventually improves the organization's success.

In conclusion, by putting people above results, servant leadership exemplifies the ideas of leading from behind. A culture of cooperation, trust, and creativity is fostered by servant leaders that prioritize the growth, development, and well-being of their teams. This change in viewpoint creates a vibrant organizational climate by empowering people to take responsibility for their tasks and transforming the leader.

6. Paying More Attention Than Talking

Effective leaders, especially those who adhere to the theory of leading from behind, must be adept at the art of listening. Gaining proficiency in active listening enables leaders to assess employee sentiment, comprehend team dynamics, and provide direction when it is most needed. Being able to actively listen is crucial in a world where there are many distractions and discussions frequently turn into monologues.

Active listening is more than just hearing what is being said; it also entails interacting with the speaker, comprehending what they are saying, and giving a considered response. To do this, leaders must put aside their personal agendas and give the speaker their full attention. Leaders communicate that their team members' opinions are important and deserving of consideration by showing genuine interest in their thoughts and feelings.

Active listening promotes a climate of psychological safety and trust, which is one of its main advantages. Employees are more inclined to voice their opinions and concerns honestly when they feel heard. Since it permits the free exchange of ideas and information, this open communication is essential for teamwork and creativity. Actively listening leaders foster an environment where team members are encouraged to participate because they know their opinions count.

Additionally, leaders who listen well are able to comprehend the distinct dynamics that exist inside their teams. Each team member contributes unique insights, difficulties, and capabilities. Leaders who listen intently can spot possible points of contention, clear up misunderstandings, and capitalize on the variety of skills present in the group. With this knowledge, leaders can better lead their teams and make sure that everyone feels appreciated and supported.

Active listening not only helps leaders understand team dynamics but also enables them to provide direction that genuinely meets the requirements of their team. Leaders should try to understand the difficulties their team members are encountering before offering answers or recommendations. In addition to fostering rapport, this sympathetic approach enables leaders to customize their support so that it speaks to the individual.

Additionally, listening shouldn't be limited to one-on-one conversations or official meetings. It is important for leaders to stay aware of the continuing discussions taking place inside their teams. Being present and involved enables leaders to get insightful information and keep an eye on team morale, whether through informal conversations during coffee breaks or team channels.

In conclusion, leaders who want to lead from behind must develop their listening skills. Leaders may improve team relationships, create a trusting environment, and offer focused assistance that genuinely meets the requirements of their staff by placing a high priority on active listening. In addition to fortifying bonds, this change in emphasis opens the door for more cooperation and creativity, which eventually propels the organization as a whole to success.

(Section III:)

Practical Leadership from Behind

7. Fostering Creativity and Innovation.

Creativity and innovation are critical for any successful business. Businesses that encourage their employees to think creatively and unconventionally stand out in today's rapidly changing world. One effective method for fostering this climate is to lead from behind, allowing others to express themselves without fear of criticism.

Psychological safety is the first step toward establishing an innovative workplace. Employees must feel safe expressing their ideas, no matter how ridiculous. Open communication, in which leaders actively accept criticism and various perspectives, contributes to this sense of security. To promote the notion that all contributions are valuable, leaders should initiate brainstorming sessions in which all ideas are encouraged.

Take Pixar, a company recognized for its innovative culture. Regular feedback sessions, known as "dailies," allow staff members to showcase their work and receive constructive comments from leaders and peers alike. The studio encourages open communication across its creative teams, emphasizing the principle that "the best ideas can come from anywhere." This strategy promotes teamwork and a sense of ownership while also boosting the quality of the final product.

Recognizing and praising creative attempts, regardless of their outcome, is another critical component of fostering innovation. When the bravery necessary to put forward fresh notions is acknowledged, the perception that taking risks is a desirable habit grows. This method is best shown by Google's "failure wall," where employees report unsuccessful attempts. Google promotes a culture that values learning from mistakes rather than hiding flaws. This mindset allows workers to push boundaries, experiment, and explore without fear of negative consequences.

Leaders must also provide innovation with the necessary time and resources to thrive. This can include designating certain hours for team members to focus on creative projects, similar to Google's "20% time" policy, which allows employees to set aside a portion of their workweek for personal pursuits. Leaders can use the power of intrinsic motivation to produce unique ideas that benefit the company by empowering team members to pursue their interests.

Finally, leaders must create a safe, encouraging environment that supports risk-taking and a range of perspectives in order to nurture innovation and creativity. Leaders may unlock their teams' full potential and propel their businesses to success by promoting open communication, recognizing innovative efforts, and providing the necessary resources.

8. Effective Delegation

The ability to delegate effectively is essential for leading from behind. Leaders who provide assignments not only reduce their workload, but also encourage their team members to embrace responsibility for their work. However, effective delegating involves a determined method that considers each team member's assets and disadvantages.

Delegating effectively begins with delegating the proper responsibilities to the right people. Leaders should spend time learning about their team members' strengths, passions, and goals. Leaders can develop a sense of accountability and ownership by assigning assignments based on individual talents. If a team member excels in data analysis, for example, assigning them a project that requires their skills will raise their confidence and benefit the organization.

After delegating duties, leaders must stay supportive without micromanaging. This equilibrium is vital. Although leaders should be available to provide guidance and aid, they must also resist the urge to take authority. Encouraging team members to carry out their responsibilities allows them to progress their careers. Leaders can stay informed without limiting their creativity by scheduling regular check-ins. Instead of prescribing how work should be done, these discussions should focus on progress, obstacles, and opportunities for growth.

Furthermore, effective delegation necessitates the exchange of constructive feedback. Feedback allows people to better understand their performance, identify areas for growth, and build their talents. Leaders should underscore the importance of learning from both positive and negative experiences. Leaders inspire their teams to achieve in their roles by building a culture of continuous development.

Effective delegating encourages both development and teamwork. Leaders can encourage teamwork by assigning projects requiring participation and feedback from multiple team members. This enhances the quality of work and strengthens team ties. When people work together to achieve a similar goal, they develop an appreciation for one other's abilities and strengths.

Finally, an important aspect of delegation is acknowledging accomplishments. Acknowledging both individual and group accomplishments helps team members to enjoy their job and emphasizes the value of collaboration. Recognizing accomplishments, whether through a formal recognition program or a simple shout-out at a team meeting, boosts motivation and fosters a feeling of community.

To summarize, effective delegation is necessary while leading from behind. Leaders can create an environment in which team members feel empowered to take responsibility for their work and contribute significantly to the company's success by assigning tasks based on individual strengths, being a supportive presence, offering constructive criticism, encouraging teamwork, and acknowledging accomplishments.

9. Managing Emergency Conditions

In times of crisis, quick action and decisive leadership are often essential. Leaders who lead from behind must find a delicate balance between remaining supportive and taking command when necessary. Effective crisis management necessitates the ability to switch between several leadership ideologies as needed.

When things are stable, leaders can empower their employees by leading from behind, which fosters independence and collaboration. However, things change when there is a crisis. Given the gravity of the situation, leaders may need to take a more active role, issuing clear orders and making critical decisions. This adjustment requires adapting the concepts of leading from behind to the current environment, rather than abandoning them.

When faced with a crisis, competent leaders assess the issue and confer with their teams. Leaders may make well-informed decisions that consider their team's experiences and insights by understanding the perspectives of those on the front lines. This method not only demonstrates how valued their thoughts are, but it also encourages teamwork and a shared aim in dealing with the crisis.

After evaluating the problem, leaders must communicate in a direct and transparent manner. Employees look to their leaders for guidance and comfort during challenging times. Regularly updating people and reacting to their concerns decreases fear while increasing trust. Leaders must be open about the challenges that lie ahead, while emphasizing the team's ability to conquer them together.

In a crisis, leaders should empower their workers to help discover a solution. Leaders may leverage their team members' diverse perspectives and abilities by including them into decision-making processes. This cooperative approach reinforces the idea that everyone can contribute to issue solving while also fostering innovation.

Leaders must remain adaptable while also empowering their teams. Because crisis situations are frequently unpredictable, it is critical to be prepared to shift direction and modify plans of action when new information becomes available. Resilience and ingenuity are critical tools for overcoming hardship, therefore leaders should encourage their employees to remain adaptable and open to change.

Finally, leaders must assess the experience once the crisis has been resolved. Debriefing sessions provide an opportunity to assess what went well and identify areas that need improvement. Leaders may build a culture of growth and resilience by acknowledging lessons learned and applauding accomplishments to better prepare their teams for future challenges.

Finally, while dealing with crises, leaders must strike a balance between decisive action and leading from behind. Leaders may effectively navigate crises while maintaining the ideals of support and collaboration by assessing the situation, communicating freely, empowering their colleagues, remaining adaptable, and reflecting on the experience.

10. Developing the Next Wave of Leaders

As organizations evolve, it becomes increasingly important to develop the next generation of leaders. In addition to boosting the firm, developing others' leadership talents ensures a long-term future in which the concept of leading from behind will persist. Organizations may build a culture of empowerment, cooperation, and creativity by investing in the development of emerging leaders.

Finding suitable people within the firm is the first step towards developing future leaders. Leaders should look for people who take initiative, want to learn, and can work well in groups. These characteristics reflect a growth mindset and a desire to take on leadership responsibilities.

Mentoring is an effective strategy for promoting the development of future leaders who have been recognized. Mentorship programs allow experienced leaders to share their knowledge, skills, and insights with emerging leaders. This collaboration improves company culture while also accelerating the development of future leaders. Mentors can assist their mentees in overcoming challenges in addition to providing constructive criticism and career advice.

Furthermore, building leadership skills necessitates the implementation of formal training and development programs. Workshops, seminars, and leadership courses can provide emerging leaders with the resources they need to succeed. Essential leadership qualities such as decision-making, communication, conflict resolution, and emotional intelligence should be the primary focus of these programs. Organizations demonstrate their commitment to the development of their future leaders by making educational investments.

Giving the next generation of leader's leadership opportunities is an important part of their growth. Giving potential leaders the opportunity to engage on projects or initiatives allows them to put their skills to use and gain valuable experiences. This practical strategy promotes self-esteem and reinforces that being a leader entails inspiring and influencing others rather than simply holding a title.

Furthermore, promoting collaboration among emerging leaders promotes a sense of belonging and shared accountability. Establishing cross-functional teams allows people to share ideas, learn from one another, and improve their leadership skills in a number of circumstances. This cooperative arrangement fosters a supportive environment and facilitates the formation of long-term partnerships.

Finally, organizations want to prioritize appreciation and feedback in their leadership development programs. While acknowledgment emphasizes positive acts and successes, regular feedback assists aspiring leaders in identifying their areas of strength and development. Celebrating triumphs and milestones encourages people to continue improving and fosters a culture of gratitude.

Finally, organizations seeking long-term success must make a considerable investment in training the next generation of executives. Organizations may create a new generation of leaders who embody the concepts of leading from behind by identifying potential leaders, providing training and mentorship, encouraging cooperation, creating opportunities for practical experience, and placing a high priority on feedback and recognition. As these emerging leaders mature, they will be more equipped to motivate others and foster an environment of empowerment, ensuring that the history of successful leadership continues for many generations.

(Section IV:)

Prospects for Leadership

11. Redefining Success: The Team, Not You, is the Key.

Redefining success to highlight group achievement is both novel and necessary in a society that usually associates leadership with individual accolades. Traditional views of successful leadership have placed a high value on individual successes such as promotions, accolades, and recognition. Leading from behind, on the other hand, challenges this way of thinking and encourages leaders to measure success via the accomplishments of their teams.

The first step toward redefining success is to recognize that good leadership is about enabling others to succeed rather than focused on one's own renown. Leaders establish a sense of community and shared purpose by prioritizing their team's accomplishments. This shift in perspective fosters collaboration and makes everyone feel invested in the organization's overall success.

Reiterating this new definition of success necessitates honoring group accomplishments. Leaders should actively acknowledge and celebrate team successes, no matter how little. This could include organizing events to recognize accomplishments, creating a "Wall of Fame" for team achievements, or publicly acknowledging individuals at meetings. Leaders promote a sense of community by recognizing the accomplishments of both individuals and groups, inspiring everyone to strive for excellence.

Leaders are also encouraged to elicit feedback from their employees when success is reframed. In addition to empowering individuals, including team members in goal-setting and decision-making processes leads to better results. When team members feel valued, they are more likely to accept responsibility for their work and contribute to a common objective.

This team-oriented technique also promotes accountability. When achievement is presented as a collaborative endeavor, team members are more likely to keep each other accountable. This camaraderie fosters a supportive environment in which people take responsibility of one another's achievements, thereby increasing engagement and productivity.

Consider the example of a sports team to exemplify this point. Although great teams frequently have star players, their success is primarily due to the collective effort and synergy of all members.

Leaders can take a cue from this model and recognize that their duty is to enable their team members collaborate and stay cohesive so that everyone has an opportunity to contribute and shine.

Furthermore, reframing success to emphasize teamwork lays the foundation for long-term growth. Organizations that prioritize group accomplishments are better able to innovate, adapt to change, and overcome challenges. This resilience is built on a solid foundation of cooperation and trust, in which team members are encouraged to take risks and explore new ideas.

To summarize, the leadership environment changes when success is reinterpreted as a collaborative endeavor. Leaders may foster an environment in which everyone feels valued and inspired to contribute to the company's success by acknowledging team accomplishments, involving team members in decision-making, and creating a culture of accountability and cooperation. True leadership in this new paradigm is determined by the team's progress and successes rather than the leader's own.

12. Establishing a Durable Legacy

A leader's influence extends far beyond their tenure in office; their legacy shapes the organization's destiny. Leading from behind not only fosters a collaborative and empowering environment, but it also establishes the foundation for the company's long-term growth and well-being. Leaders must consciously examine the principles they wish to instill in their teams as well as the legacy they want to leave behind.

Creating a strong corporate culture founded on shared values is the first step towards leaving a lasting legacy. Leaders inspire their staff to adopt these ideals by modeling appropriate behavior. Long after the leader has left, this alignment produces a shared sense of purpose that guides actions and decisions. For example, a leader who prioritizes honesty and openness will most likely urge their team to do the same, creating an environment that values responsibility and honesty.

Funding the training of future leaders is also an important part of leaving a legacy. Leaders ensure the continuation of their vision and goals by instilling leadership qualities in others. The next generation of leaders must be prepared through mentoring, training courses, and opportunities for advancement. When given the authority to carry on the company's legacy, emerging leaders become guardians of the culture and strengthen its core values.

Encouraging diversity and inclusiveness inside the organization is another critical component of leaving a legacy. Leaders who embrace a variety of perspectives not only encourage innovation, but also contribute to a more equitable workplace. A legacy that values inclusion ensures that everyone's perspectives are acknowledged and heard, creating an environment in which people from diverse backgrounds can thrive.

Leaders should emphasize the importance of social responsibility and community involvement. Businesses that prioritize social responsibility and actively contribute in their communities have a beneficial ripple effect that reaches beyond their local operations. Leaders ensure that their legacy includes a commitment to transforming the world by instilling these values in the very fiber of the organization.

Starbucks' history under former CEO Howard Schultz illustrates this viewpoint. By incorporating these values into the company's operations, Schultz focused on creating an inclusive and socially responsible culture. Starbucks is now recognized for its commitment to ethical sourcing and community involvement, in addition to its coffee.

The company's operations and the beliefs it promotes are clear examples of this legacy, demonstrating that leadership is about creating a positive impact rather than just making money.

Finally, leaders must embrace an attitude of continuous adaptability and progress. To thrive, organizations must adapt to a constantly changing world. Leaders ensure that their legacy is one of adaptability and resilience by cultivating a culture of learning and innovation. This type of thinking allows groups to see change and barriers as opportunities for growth, setting the groundwork for long-term success.

Finally, in order to establish a lasting impact as a leader, you must employ a broad strategy. Leaders may leave a lasting legacy by cultivating a strong company culture, investing in the next generation of leaders, promoting diversity and inclusion, prioritizing social responsibility, and embracing continuous improvement. In addition to influencing the organization's future, this legacy inspires following generations of leaders to uphold the leadership from behind tenets, ensuring that the organization's beliefs and mission live on for a long time.

Conclusion: The Way Ahead

As we conclude this inquiry into leading from behind, it is critical that we evaluate the paths each of us might take to become leaders who empower others. In a rapidly changing world, traditional leadership ideals are under attack. There has never been a greater demand for leaders that prioritize people, teamwork, and collective achievement. The time has arrived for you to embrace this paradigm shift in order to inspire and grow others around you while also improving your leadership style.

Developing a "Behind the Scenes" Leader's Mindset
Adopting the mindset of a leader who leads from behind is the first stage in this process. It requires making the purposeful decision to prioritize the

needs of your team, realizing that your role is to be the stage manager who ensures that everyone else shines, rather than the star of the show. This mentality change requires being present, actively listening, and knowing the dynamics within your team.

Think about your leadership style for a moment. Do you frequently find yourself at the center of attention? When your team is given the opportunity to lead, do you step forward quickly? Admitting one's inclinations is the first step toward transformation. Instead, consider how you can empower people around you.

Gather feedback from your team and learn what they think about leadership. Create open conversation venues where team members can share ideas on how to improve efficiency and cooperation. Use this knowledge as a resource for your leadership development. This not only builds trust, but also demonstrates your commitment to taking the initiative.

Empowerment Tools

The foundation of leading from behind is empowerment. It all boils down to giving your staff the resources they need to succeed. The following are some strategies you may apply right now to establish an environment that empowers individuals.

Promote Autonomy: Assign roles and responsibilities so that team members can take responsibility for their own work. Have faith in their ability to make decisions and provide aid without interference. This independence fosters self-confidence and inventiveness.

Provide Training and Resources: Invest in the professional development of your employees.

Provide workshops, training sessions, and materials to help them grow professionally. This increases their abilities and demonstrates that you are concerned about their achievement.

Recognize Contributions: Continue to recognize your team members for their accomplishments and hard work. Recognize successes of all sizes and promote a culture of gratitude. Acknowledgment encourages further participation and reinforces the value of each individual's contributions.

Encourage Open Communication: Create a climate in which team members can freely express their ideas, concerns, and criticisms. Make it clear that every voice matters, and encourage conversation and active listening.

Set a positive example for your team by acting in the ways that you expect them to perform. Be accountable, honest, and open in your behavior.

When you demonstrate these characteristics, your staff will be more likely to emulate you.

Creating a Helpful Network

Creating a network of allies within your organization is another component of leading from behind. Interact with other leaders who share your vision for a team-oriented leadership approach. Working together, you can create a culture that values trust, empowerment, and group achievement.

Consider forming peer mentorship groups to help leaders share their experiences and methods for leading from behind. Leaders who commit to this method can foster a feeling of community and obtain valuable insights from these groups.

Look for opportunities to collaborate amongst departments as well. Encourage groups to work together on initiatives, breaking down organizational silos and promoting the sharing of resources and ideas. This encourages innovation and reinforces the sense that success requires a collaborative effort.

Turning Your Attention to Group Achievement

As you embark on this journey, keep in mind that the ultimate goal is to shift your focus from individual recognition to communal achievement. This requires a big change in your organization's performance measures. Make it a practice to highlight team accomplishments and the collaborative work that led to them rather than celebrating individual achievements.

Consider implementing team-based performance criteria that prioritize cooperation and group results. Some examples include group objectives, mutual rewards, and teamwork-recognition campaigns. This reinterpretation of success assists to reaffirm that everyone is necessary to achieve organizational goals.

Developing the Upcoming Leadership Generation

One of the most essential things a leader can do is to shape the next generation. Investing in the training of future leaders not only ensures the continuance of your vision but also has a long-term impact.

Encourage mentoring inside your firm by pairing experienced team members with those looking to improve their leadership skills. In addition to instilling a sense of community, this offers aspiring leaders the confidence to embrace the concept of leading from behind.

Provide opportunities for leadership development projects that focus on empowerment, empathy, and teamwork. Give prospective leaders the tools they need to succeed in today's fast-changing environment. This commitment to creating leadership will have long-term benefits, establishing a legacy of talented personnel who can propel the organization forward.

The trip goes on

Remember that becoming a leader who empowers others is an ongoing process. It requires a commitment to lifelong learning, growth, and adaptation. Be open to criticism and preserve your flexibility. Being adaptable will be critical to your success in today's ever-changing leadership landscape.

Reflect on the knowledge you gained from studying leadership from behind. Use them as a framework to help you grow as a leader. Remember that your success is inextricably related to the success of those you lead; embrace the power of collaboration and cultivate an environment of empowerment and trust.

In conclusion, major change is required to move forward. By committing to lead from behind, you may enhance the lives of others around you while also changing the perception of leadership. Working together, you can create a future where empowerment, teamwork, and everyone's success are the hallmarks of leadership. This is the legacy of a true leader, one who will inspire future generations.

Call to action

Appreciate you reading! I would want to take a moment to personally thank you for selecting to read my work. Your time and effort are much valued; perhaps, this book will give you insightful analysis and successful techniques.

Your comments are very much valued as I develop as an author. I would love to hear your thoughts—whether positive or constructive—so I can improve and make future works even more helpful and engaging.

 I respectfully ask that you write an honest review whether you thought this book was beneficial or if you could see anything improved. Your observations will not only help me but also guide other readers toward appropriate materials.

I appreciate your support once more; I am looking forward your comments. Good wishes,

Lead from Behind

Lead from Behind

www.ingramcontent.com/pod-product-compliance
Lightning Source LLC
Chambersburg PA
CBHW070211230526
45471CB00002B/925